MW00834645

JOHN TRAVOLTA

by
Suzanne Munshower

Edited by
Barbara Williams Prabhu

Grosset & Dunlap
A Filmways Company
Publishers • New York

JOHN TRAVOLTA
Adapted from the book MEET JOHN TRAVOLTA
Abridged from The John Travolta Scrapbook
Copyright © 1976, 1978 by Suzanne Munshower
ISBN: 0-448-16498-1
Library Edition ISBN: 0-448-26270-3
Library of Congress Catalog Card No.: 78-59480
Published simultaneously in Canada
Printed in the United States of America

Photo by Shaun Considine - Globe Photos

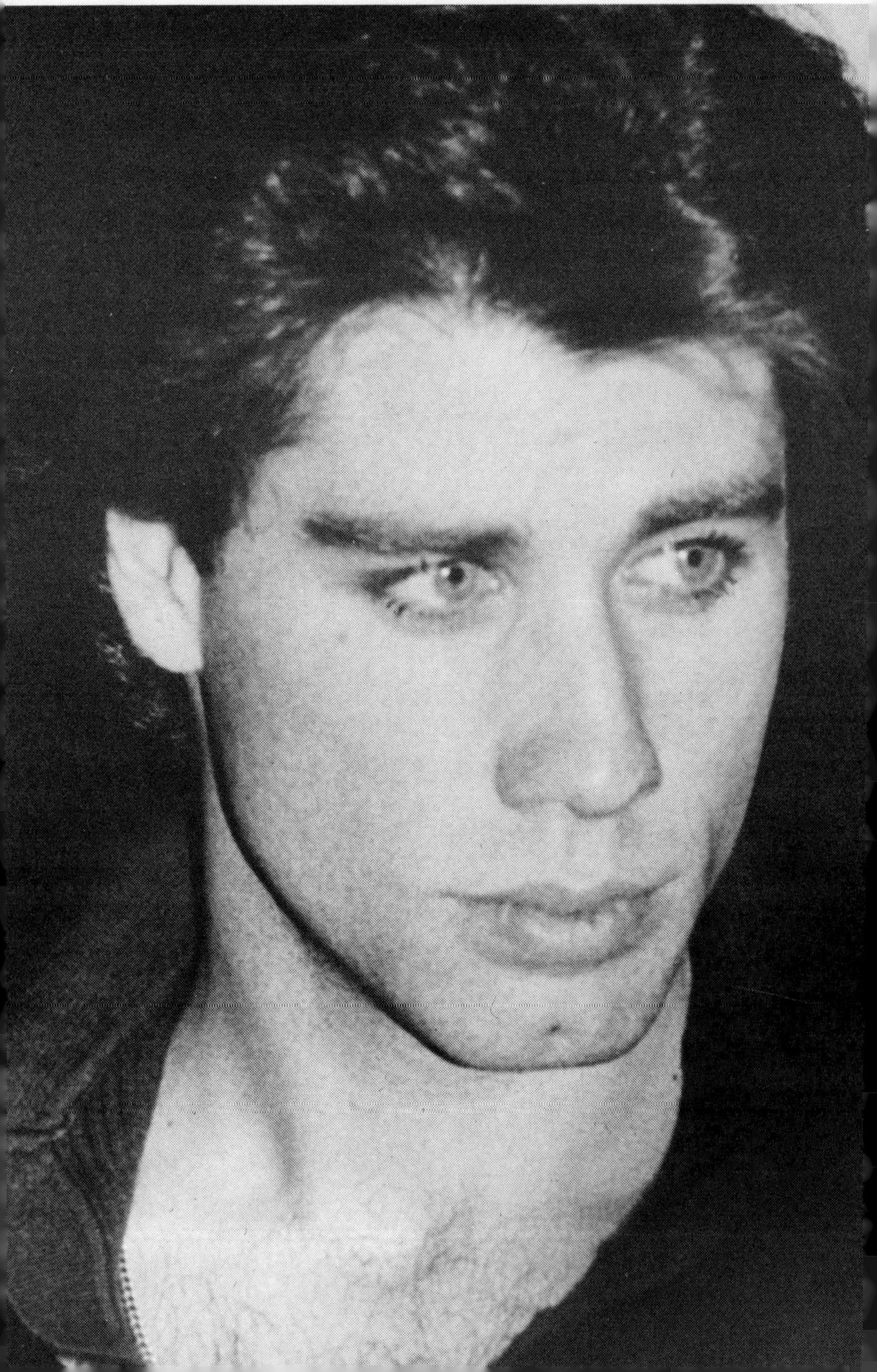

1

Good Looks, Talent and Charisma

He is, in a word, fantastic! Young girls love him; young boys think he's cool; and adults admire his looks and talent. Is there anyone who *isn't* crazy about John Travolta? Some days it seems the answer is no.

Until he signed a contract to play Vinnie Barbarino on the weekly TV comedy series "Welcome Back, Kotter," John Travolta was simply an actor who few people had ever heard of.

Although his career may seem like the classic case of overnight success, he has been making a living appearing on stage, on TV, and in movies since he was 16 years old.

A writer who met with John before he became a star on "Welcome Back, Kotter" remembers a boy who was totally unlike Vinnie Barbarino, the character John portrays on the show. As a matter of fact, she remembers John as a very shy young man.

"He was open and perfectly willing to talk," she recalls, "but it was obvious he didn't feel totally at ease. He was very shy and he spoke in this soft little voice. I felt sure then and there that he'd be a big star one day.

"Why did I feel that way? Well, it wasn't just that he was such a nice person or that he seemed happy to go out of his way to be nice and pleasant and

John Travolta with Anita Gillette, in the 1976 production of *Bus Stop*. Photo by Frank Teti

The "Welcome Back, Kotter" gang. *Top l-r:* Ron Palillo, Robert Hegyes. *Bottom l-r:* John Travolta, Gabe Kaplan and Lawrence Jacobs.
UPI

helpful. It was more that he had this incredible charisma, the real stuff of which stars are made.

"John would open those startling blue eyes and look so *innocent*! Frankly, I was surprised when I'd heard he'd been cast as Barbarino. It seemed like such an aggressive role for a nice boy like John."

It's hard to believe that not too long ago, John Travolta was what's known in show business as a "nobody." Today he's probably *the* most popular young actor in the United States.

By the summer of 1976, it was no longer a great shock that John had to be whisked away from anxious mobs of fans who surrounded him when he was appearing in shops to promote his record album. On one occasion, there were so many screaming admirers that John had to be spirited out of a major department store disguised as a local policeman!

Certainly, it's no surprise that John is in so much demand for everything these days—personal appearances, performances, interviews, autographs—that he can afford to say "no" to anything that doesn't meet his terms. Right now John is successful enough to be able to call all the shots.

Some of John's success comes from being in the right show at the right time. In the early 1970s there was a shortage of teenage stars. Donny and Marie Osmond were *the* teen idols in America, with little competition.

And then there was Henry Winkler who portrayed Arthur Fonzarelli on "Happy Days." Kids were starved for a favorite, and "The Fonz" was a new breed of teen star. He wasn't all sunshine and lollipops like David Cassidy or Donny Osmond. The Fonz was not cute and clean-cut; he was a slightly grubby, tough-talking guy who didn't take garbage from anyone. He was always good for a laugh, and The Fonz was appealing. He was even nice enough to meet with approval from the strictest of parents. Why? Because he was just—The Fonz.

Teenagers responded like crazy! Soon everyone was copying The Fonz. Still, though, the new idol didn't satisfy *all* teens, and when Vinnie Barbarino came along in "Kotter," the time was ripe.

John Travolta's reputation as the top teen idol was confirmed when he started getting more fan mail than Henry Winkler. He's swamped with letters every day—about 5,000 a week. John has said his mail is "mostly from girls between the ages of 13 and 18. They write a great deal about love."

But boys *and* girls, as well as adults, have been buying the tee-shirts, tote bags, postcards, posters and magazines that display John's picture. In a

Karen Gorney and John Travolta play two
youths trying to escape the roles society has
set up for them in *Saturday Night Fever*. Photo
Trends

very short time his name has become a household word and his face has become familiar to everyone.

There's no doubt about it—John Travolta's popularity has vaulted him to the status of superstar. With *Saturday Night Fever* and *Grease* making him one of the top box office draws of the 1970s, his future is assured.

What has made John Travolta a superstar? Most folks agree it's a combination of good looks, talent, charisma and hard work.

John is a clean-cut, great-looking guy. He's just over six feet tall. His body is slim without being skinny, muscular without being musclebound. His dark brown hair is thick and shiny. His face has a straight nose, a cleft in the chin, a square jaw and intense blue eyes. Many say those piercing eyes are his most striking feature, others believe it's the way he carries himself—with assur-

Getting made up for *Saturday Night Fever*.

ance and confidence. Whatever his physical appeal, it blends the best of his "Italian-Irish" heritage.

John definitely didn't have to rely on his looks when it came to winning the role of Vinnie Barbarino in "Welcome Back, Kotter." And looks alone didn't win him the role of Tony Manero in *Saturday Night Fever* or Danny Zuko in *Grease*. His acting talent won those roles for him. And once John gets

a role, the mixture of looks, talent and charisma that is John Travolta, takes over.

So now John is a star, an idol. With everyone watching him all the time, he has learned that a star must be careful of whatever he says and does. John talked about his influence over his fans in an article in *People* magazine:

"I'd taken a publicity picture wearing a shirt with mismatching buttons on the cuffs," he said. "Now my agent's niece says all her friends in junior high are wearing mismatching buttons on their shirts. People should be careful about the advice they give others. I'm definitely an opinion maker."

Because he learned this lesson early in his career, John tries to keep a low profile with his fans. He doesn't say all kids should do the same as he did when he was their age. And he doesn't preach Scientology—his chosen religion—

either. John is careful about the advice he gives to others.

Instead of showing off, he's busy enjoying his career and his new way of life. He no longer lives with his parents in Englewood, New Jersey. Now he has his own apartment in a suburb of Los Angeles. He owns his own plane and has a private pilot's license. He dates lots of girls and plans to marry and settle down some day. He comes from a closely-knit family and spends as much time as he can with his parents, his three sisters and two brothers.

In some ways, John Travolta sounds a lot like the rest of us, and that's one of the things that's so great about him: He's a regular guy. He's just like the kid next door, or down the block. Knowing he's a lot like the rest of us lets us in on one of the reasons why John is so popular. And that's important.

2
Getting It Together

John Travolta is now, and has always been, very much his own person. As far as he's concerned, everyone must make his or her own choices in life. A major choice John made in his own life shows not only his self-confidence, but the love and respect that exists between John and his parents.

The youngest of six children, John grew up in Englewood, New Jersey, an older community with fine-looking brick and clapboard houses, manicured front lawns, and clean streets that show the pride of the residents. Englewood boasts a high percentage of commuters, people who go into Manhattan every day to work, but prefer a quieter neighborhood to live in.

"I wanted to quit high school and go into acting full time," he recalls. "I told my father about my wishes—and he was shocked. But he made a deal with me. He said that I could leave school for a year—if everything worked out and I could make money, I wouldn't have to go back. But he made me promise that if I didn't succeed, I would be back at Dwight Morrow High School the next year."

John was doing summer stock in New Jersey that year, and had an offer to open in another show in the fall. But,

UPI

18

he was also due to go into eleventh grade at the same time. So he made the deal with his dad. He's proud to say "everything went so well, that after that, it didn't matter."

By leaving school, John was able to accept roles and traveling assignments that schoolbound teenage actors were forced to turn down. However, he doesn't attempt to influence younger people into quitting high school. If anything, he tries to convince them to stay in school. He admits that his was a purely individual decision.

John doesn't feel high school is a waste of time. He says seriously, "I don't think kids in the tenth grade should drop out because I did. In fact, I wouldn't want to see my own children quit school. It's very important for kids to complete their education. I've been exceptionally lucky. But I want other kids to realize that it would be extremely foolish for them to drop out of school and count on luck to pull them through."

John was lucky to have parents who understood his ambitions and encouraged them. He was lucky to be able to study with the best teachers, with people who could train his natural talents. John was also lucky to be spotted by an agent who took great interest in his early career, guiding him and giving him wise advice on every professional move.

John feels that having an early career helped him avoid some of the problems the average teenager is forced to face, like the drug problem. When drugs and what they are doing to young Americans are discussed, John is quick to praise his career for having kept him away from drugs.

Music will never lose its place in John's heart. He's an expert singer and dancer and a capable musician. But, he insists that his acting career will never take a back seat to anything in his life. Jim McHugh - Sygma

Of his own experiences, John remembers: "I was in high school when that was getting pretty popular. I remember the most popular athletes being killed by overdoses, and they were guys with really incredible abilities. And yet, it was just an outside force that sort of came in and contaminated the whole school." How did John escape drug use?

"I knew I didn't like it. I knew it wasn't going to help me, and I felt uncomfortable even thinking about it. But also, I was not in with a group of people who were into that kind of stuff."

John admits that the threat was never really great—not as far as he was concerned. "I don't think any of my close friends ever got heavily involved in drugs," he says, "when I was there at least. But you knew who the users were. There were always ways to avoid getting involved."

Today John continues to turn thumbs down on drugs of any kind. He feels that drugs help keep people down and don't make them grow in any way. "That's the hard part," he explains in discussing drug users. "The odds are against those who are into drugs. And if they only knew there are so many better ways to go. It doesn't have to be acting, it doesn't have to be Scientology as it is for me, but there are ways."

For John, when he was 16, the answer was show business. The entertainment world has been more than a salvation or even a way of life for John. It's become his life.

John doesn't plan on going back to school because he is very involved in his religion—Scientology. He believes Scientology helps him deal with his life better and that it helps him to understand his own mind and everyone elses. John says, "What I'm

learning in Scientology is helping me study, too."

Scientology was founded in 1950 by L. Ron Hubbard, an American writer of science fiction who claims to have

Photo by Frank Teti

found a way to help people cure themselves of their problems. John credits much of his level-headedness to its teachings.

Although John has chosen Scientology for himself, he feels that whatever works for others is what's good for them. Although he doesn't preach, he does see what he calls "a major change in consciousness" occurring all over the world. "Everybody is coming to an awareness," he says, "that if they want to help themselves and they think something is going to help them, they can do it."

John is certainly doing it. He believes that a person can accomplish anything he or she is determined to do, and this attitude is reflected in his successful career.

3

Making It To Broadway

His family and his career are the most important things in John Travolta's life. And he freely says so.

"Sure," he's said, "there's nothing I like better than talking about the people I love. I have a great family—my mother, Helen, is an actress and director herself, so I guess you could say I was brought up on show business—though not here in Hollywood. My dad, Salvatore, owns a large tire shop back

John's parents visited him backstage when he was appearing in the summer stock perform- ance of *Bus Stop*. Photo by Frank Teti

in New Jersey and he used to play pro- fessional football.

"I've got a brother Joe, who is older than I am, but some people say we could pass for twins. Two of my sisters are in show business, too. One does voice commercials and the other has her own local talk show in Palm Springs."

All three Travolta boys and the three Travolta girls have acted and have appeared on television commercials. It's almost the family business.

"We always had enough," John recalls, "but we were by no means well off. We lived in a big house in Englewood and had lots of love. All the kids worked by the time we were 12 or 13, because we didn't want to be a burden to our parents."

Before John's folks got married, his mother, Helen Burke, was a member of a group called the Sunshine Sisters. After their marriage, Mrs. Travolta didn't lose her interest in show business, but kept very busy with local theater groups.

His mother's interest in theater was so great that " . . . the result was like dominoes—the oldest of her children got interested in acting . . . and the next . . . and the next one. . . . It was the accepted thing in our family to perform. You were either interested in sports, because my father was an athlete, or you were interested in theater," John says.

Born on February 18, 1954, John grew up surrounded by older brothers and sisters who were working in show business. Consequently, he was subjected to the excitement of the theater at a very early age. It gave his mother's show business influence added weight.

Actually, it was inevitable that John would develop an interest in getting his share of the limelight, especially after seeing how happy theatrical careers made others in his own family.

John's sisters Ann and Ellen were part of a show business revival recently. They appeared with their kid brother and his co-star Anita Gillette in a straw hat tour of the play *Bus Stop*. Besides this, Ann (or "Annie," as John affectionately calls her) appeared alongside her brother on Broadway in the hit musical *Grease* and did a small part in the move *Saturday Night Fever*. Ellen has her own talk show in Palm Springs, California, and frequently appears in television series. And John's third sister Margaret, is active doing television commercials in Chicago, Illinois, where she lives. It certainly seems like show business *is* the family business.

John made his own amateur theatrical debut in 1966 when he was 12, appearing with his mother in a local New Jersey production of *Who'll Save The Plowboy?* He got experience for his performance, but no pay! So, by the time John left school at 16, he had four years of acting experience.

His first professional acting job was also in New Jersey. He received $50 a week for playing the lead in *Bye Bye Birdie*. A talent agent named Bob LeMond saw him there and has been with John ever since. It's unusual for a teenager to acquire an agent, especially during his first professional engagement. This shows how things began going well for John right from the start.

Every serious young actor puts time into summer stock. John spent a season at the Allanbury Playhouse in Pennsylvania, where he appeared in two musical comedies, *The Boyfriend* and *She*

A moment's discussion with another family member, John's sister, Ellen. Photo by Frank Teti

Loves Me. He thought it was great to sing and dance and take home a paycheck for it. Still a teenager, John was happy to be getting professional work—it's not an easy profession to break into and John knew it.

Once John had decided to become an actor, he began commuting from Englewood to New York City, a short drive aross the George Washington Bridge, where he took lessons in acting, dance and voice.

With Bob LeMond guiding his career, John began to do a number of TV commercials. What was it like doing his first commercials? "I was very excited," John recalls. "To see yourself on TV is really something neat. And I went from getting $50 a week to getting over $1,000. That was unreal at the time. As for how I feel about commercials now, the difference is that I'm offered $50,000 for them!"

John worked very hard during these early years. When he wasn't actually on stage, he was busy studying or practicing, or making TV commercials. He read scripts, studied lines, did his musical scales, danced to keep in shape, and of course, he made the rounds.

He would read for this part or that part, audition for this commercial, that play, this showcase. He would travel to New York to meet with casting directors, to learn what was going on, to find out what parts were available.

It was about this time John got a role in an off-Broadway play called *Metaphors*. His good looks, talent and charm made him ideal for all sorts of roles. The following year he appeared in *Rain*, and in revivals of *Gypsy* and *Bye Bye Birdie*.

John then joined the national touring company of *Grease*, one of America's favorite musicals. He played a character named "Doodie," a sort of dizzy, well-meaning kid, who is the

youngest, dopiest member of a gang. After nine months with the company, John was invited to portray "Doodie" on Broadway!

Broadway! John was only 18 at the time! This early success proved his parents had made the right choice when they permitted him to leave school to work on his career.

Things kept moving along in an upward direction for young Travolta. He could play the innocent kid or the suave young man. With his adaptability and his eagerness to try everything the theater had to offer, John found his scope as an actor constantly expanding. He was learning his craft in the

Olivia Newton-John joins John Travolta at a party for the opening of the 1977 production of *Grease*. Photo by Frank Edwards - Fotos International

Left: John sang and danced with Patti Andrews in the Broadway hit *Over Here! Right:* John as the Disco King in *Saturday Night Fever.* UPI

best way of all—by constant practice and hard work.

One Broadway success was soon followed by another. For eight months John appeared in the musical *Over Here!*, starring Patti and Maxene Andrews of the 1940's singing trio, the Andrews Sisters.

When John was in Los Angeles with the touring company of *Grease* he had decided Hollywood was where it was really at. So, when *Over Here!* closed, he packed his bags and moved to the West Coast.

But John Travolta knew that he wasn't just moving from one coast to another. For an actor on the East Coast, appearing in a successful Broadway play is tops, and John had been in two! He'd had that experience and was now ready to break into the Hollywood scene.

4

Joining A
Television Family

J ohn threw himself into this new
phase of his career just as any
nose-to-the-grindstone East Coast work-
aholic might. He spent his days visiting
casting directors and auditioning, his
nights with his family and friends
planning his future. His efforts paid
off—he became a member of the "Kotter"
family.

"Welcome Back, Kotter" was first
seen on ABC-TV on September 9, 1975.

The idea for the series came from Gabe Kaplan, a successful TV and nightclub comedian.

There are few people in the United States today who don't know who Gabriel Kaplan is. But, it hasn't always been that way. In 1974, Gabe appeared at Caesar's Palace in Las Vegas as the opening act for Paul Anka. The audience had come to hear Anka sing. They had never seen Gabe Kaplan before, but by the time he finished his stand-up comic routines all the people were murmuring, "Hey, this guy's good!"

Whereas John admits that roles just came his way as an actor and that there was never anything else he wanted to be, for Gabe, success was not easy. Gabe didn't realize he wanted to be a comic until after he had dropped out of high school.

Gabriel Kaplan was born in the

Crown Heights section of Brooklyn, New York, where his parents still live. His father, Charles Kaplan, was a real estate salesman, his mother Dorothy, a beautician. Gabe takes great pride in his Jewish ethnic heritage, often referring to it in his comedy routines.

Like John, Gabe left home soon after quitting school. He wasn't sure of what he wanted out of life, but he knew that Crown Heights didn't offer what he was looking for. For Gabe, being on his own was an uphill climb. His first occupation was that of a ball player. He was a left fielder in the minor leagues. After quitting the baseball circuit, Gabe worked as a hotel bellhop. It was while working at a hotel in New Jersey that Gabe started watching the comics performing in the hotel's nightclub.

So, Gabe started getting his act together and playing his stand-up routines. Finally he discovered what he liked doing best in life; he had found his career. He was happy being a stand-up comic.

Soon, Gabe realized that of all his comedy routines, those drawn from characters of the kids he had grown up with in Brooklyn were the most popular. He thought about putting those kids into a television series, brought his ideas to some people in Hollywood, and they bought it!

The show was planned around a hip teacher, Gabe Kotter, to be played by creator Gabriel Kaplan. The "sweathogs"—a gang of tough high school kids—were all seen as equally interesting. They were a bunch of wise guys, doing all the crazy things and making all the crazy mistakes most kids make trying to get through high school.

Before the show had its debut, producer James Komack talked about it with the press: "It's basically the story of a borderline delinquent from a poor section, stuck in an inept school system, who somehow makes his way and gets his teacher's degree.

"And where does he wind up? Right back in the school he struggled to escape from, but this time teaching social studies and remedial reading. The kids haven't changed. They're still poor, estranged from society and as apt to insult a teacher as say 'hello' to one. Naturally, we'll reflect the prevailing language of the streets, or as much of it as we're able to on TV. But, Kotter, as our teacher's called, can't forget his past and he knows instinctively how to deal with the kids.

"We went to New York and picked four naturals to play the main student parts. Only one has any real acting credits. They're perfect for what we want to show—what goes on in a classroom in a poor section of town.

"Everybody connected with the production of the show grew up in New York, so we all know the story," Komack concluded.

Even before the debut of the series, the word got around Hollywood circles that producer Komack was being pressed to dress up the show a little, to make it cuter and milder, and less like the real-life atmosphere of an inner city high school. But Komack stood firm. He liked the show the way it was, and he had no intention of pushing his writers into changing it to make anyone else happy. He wouldn't weaken.

"I can tell you this," he promised potential viewers, " 'Welcome Back,

Kotter' will be the real thing, the way a poor school is now. The language won't be pretty, but it'll be honest."

Komack's strength worked. The show succeeded, and interestingly enough, "Kotter" has grown in the direction of a gentler gang of kids. Today they aren't nearly as tough and as street-wise as they were three years ago when the show started. The "sweathogs" have mellowed with age and have become *nicer*.

The "sweathogs" are Juan Epstein (Robert Hegyes), Arnold Horshack (Ron Palillo), Freddie "Boom-Boom" Washington (Larry Jacobs), and of course, Vinnie Barbarino (better known as John Travolta). Vinnie is leader of the pack, the idol of James Buchanan High School.

Unlike some of the others chosen for the series, John at 20 was a seasoned professional. And the audience response recognized this. Soon the series was billed as "the show that features John Travolta as Vinnie Barbarino." John was one of the major reasons for the show's tremendous popularity.

John has never been one to hog the limelight. He knows the other young actors on the series worked just as hard as he and paid their own dues in the acting profession. But John couldn't help the fact that the viewers liked him best from the very start. That's just the way it was and John knew it.

"I didn't quite expect the show to be the hit it is," John admits in dazed surprise. "I didn't think it could get to be this big. It's crazy!" Maybe, but the success is *real*, too. And the girls that scream and yell, and follow him home are *real*.

John says, "I remember at the audition, I said to myself, 'Gee, if I can pull this one off, I'm doing pretty well.'

"I didn't think of myself as being the macho type. On the stage, I've always been cast in the meekest types of roles, in *The Misfits, Grease,* and *Over Here!* I didn't think the producers would believe I could play the role of Vinnie. But I guess I was wrong."

Yes, happily for all of us, John was wrong; the producers decided he was perfect for the role of Vinnie Barbarino. Still, it hasn't been easy for him to adjust to his new role as a top teen idol.

John says he's given his new public image a great deal of thought. For a while there he wasn't sure whether folks were reacting to John Travolta the actor, or "Vinnie Barbarino," the character. But he also says that he loved the role of Vinnie from the start. "I got so excited about the part because it was well written and I immediately identified with the kind of person Vinnie was," he says. "He was so easy to do! I just knew that character!"

Every actor has had to deal with the fact that many fans confuse the actors with the characters they play. This is something each has to adjust to. After all, everyone wants to be appreciated for the person they really are, not for some make-believe character dreamed up by a group of writers.

Most of the "Kotter" cast share the same feelings about their roles, and about each other. As Larry Jacobs puts it: "The five of us have a trust for each other, a genuine love for each other, so we work as a unit." Being able to work well with others is essential to show business, and part of John Travolta's success is due to his ability to do so.

John speaks of his experience on

"Kotter" as "the best time I've ever had," and there isn't one of the "sweathogs" who doesn't agree with him. They all feel the same way about the series and each other, and as actors, they all have the same hopes and fears, too.

When speaking of his fellow "sweathogs," John says, "I like all of them. I love all the guys, but Larry and I go out to a movie or have dinner together and talk more often."

What is John's friend, Lawrence-Hilton Jacobs like?

Larry was born in New York City, one of nine children of Clothilda and Hilton Jacobs. Since he comes from such a big family, he can share many of John's memories of growing up with a lot of other people around.

Like John, Larry never wanted to be anything except an actor. He has held other jobs—delivery boy, stock boy, gas station attendant, florist, free-lance artist, messenger, package designer— in his life, in addition to his acting. But he says, "I always wanted to be an actor, ever since I was in diapers.

"But I had to stay with my family; they were against the idea. But I think their attitude was good for me; it gave me a challenge, made me try harder. . . . All I know is that from my earliest memories, I thought of nothing but going into this work and making it my life's work.

"At 15 I bought the trade papers, saw where they were holding auditions, and went and tried for roles," Larry says. "Sure I was scared, and many times I was unsuccessful, but you have to fall down because it gives you something to shoot for."

It wasn't long before Larry was

working on commercials. Then his first big break—he was signed to work with the respected Al Fann Theatrical Ensemble. The next step was the renowned Negro Ensemble Company, and from then on, everything was roses for the handsome six-foot-two, 163-pound actor.

Larry has appeared in quite a few films. He has had small roles in *The Gambler, Serpico, Death Wish,* and *Supercops,* and featured parts in *Claudine* and *Cooley High*. It's interesting that another unknown actor also had a bit part in *Serpico*—Robert Hegyes, who now plays "Juan Louis Pedro Phillip de Huevos Epstein," in "Welcome Back, Kotter."

Bob Hegyes, who was born in Perth Amboy, New Jersey—not far from John's home town of Englewood—hasn't got any Spanish blood in him.

The Latin blood he does have is Italian, mixed with some Hungarian.

The five-foot-seven, 160-pound actor also hails from a relatively large family. He's the eldest of four children of Steven and Marie Hegyes.

Bob wasn't sure whether he wanted to be an actor or a teacher when he graduated from Wilkes College in Wilkes Barre, Pennsylvania, but he had a whole collection of majors— speech, theater and education—in his Bachelor of Arts degree. Bob met his wife, Mary Eileen Kunes, at school where she was majoring in microbiology.

Like John, Bob was lucky to have folks who supported his acting ambitions. He says, "My parents, and more importantly, my wife, were very encouraging. We were married before I set out to be an actor, and when I first started going to New York, she was working at a hospital, which enabled me to get into New York every night."

It was very important for Bob that Mary was a liberated wife with a career of her own. Bob was working on and off Broadway, gathering credits and valuable experience as an actor, but sometimes earning as little as $20 a performance. "But I was working, and I was learning," he says of those days.

The role of Juan Epstein came along at just the right time for Bob. "I tested for the role back in New York," he recalls. "I was doing a Broadway show at the time called *Don't Call Back*, and it closed in one night. But it closed on the same night that I found out I got my role on 'Kotter.' It was neat."

Ron Palillo feels the same way about his role as the now-beloved Arnold Horshack. The five-foot-seven,

120-pound actor was born in New Haven, Connecticut. His father Gabriel died when Ron was only nine years old, and his mother Carmen is now retired.

Ron says that with two older brothers and a sister, all professionals, "I was the bum of the family because I always wanted to be in the theater. And everyone in my family said, 'No way are you going to pursue a career as an actor.'

"Well, I started my own theater when I was about 14 and it was pretty well done. It was kind of a glorified community theater." Ron says he wasn't surprised when his theater turned out to be a huge success, both critically and financially. It was a real thrill for him, of course.

"I got to play all of the parts I ever wanted to play because I was running it, directing it, doing the publicity, the whole number!" Ron was such a good actor that he won a scholarship to the University of Connecticut, and graduated with a Bachelor of Fine Arts degree in theater arts. After graduation he did a stint at Player Repertory in Miami, then left for New York City. While appearing on Broadway in the play *Hot L Baltimore* Ron read for the role of Arnold Horshack for the "Welcome Back, Kotter" people.

Ron went to the audition thinking he didn't have a chance at the part. When Gabe Kaplan and Helen Sacks saw Ron they said "If you can act, you've got the part." And Ron thought "Boy, do I have them fooled, they think I'm tough." After reading the script Ron was still confused about how he should play the role.

"Finally, I just said, 'Hello, how are you? I'm Arnold Horshack,' in almost the same manner I'd deliver the line today," Ron recalls, "and they laughed.

"Well, I still wasn't sure of myself, and after the audition, as I started to leave, I was so nervous that I walked into the door, and they kind of laughed, and I thought that I had blown the whole thing. But a couple of days later, I was told I got the part."

Today, Ron is another happy and satisfied "sweathog," and one of John's closest friends.

John Travolta has Larry Jacobs, Bob Hegyes and Ron Palillo to buddy around with. And he relates to Gabe Kaplan on a work-oriented level. The five men also share interests in sports, frequently meeting to play out a brisk game of basketball or tennis.

The "sweathogs" see a lot of each other both on and off duty. They're really friends, and they know they can count on each other. They are more than just a bunch of co-stars. They're people who come from much the same backgrounds; people who really understand one another. It's a group effort all the way.

And this group has become sort of a second family to John Travolta. No matter what occurs in his future, John says there'll always be a place in his life for the special friends he has made through "Welcome Back, Kotter."

5

Reaching The Stars

Although John Travolta achieved success through "Welcome Back, Kotter," his contract wasn't handed to him as he got off the New York plane in Los Angeles. He first had to make the name *John Travolta* known to West Coast casting directors and producers.

He did this as any other aspiring actor does—by making the rounds, auditioning and being interviewed. Of course, John had help from his sister

Ellen and his agent Bob LeMond. Even before his audition for "Kotter," John was breaking into the movieland scene.

John made his movie debut in a horror film, *The Devil's Rain*, starring Ernest Borgnine, Ida Lupino and Eddie Albert. They filmed on location in Mexico. This minor role gave John the chance to work with pros in the movie side of show business.

Also, *The Devil's Rain*, even if it wasn't exactly Academy Award material, was a fun film. It was an old-fashioned kind of horror story about hideously deformed murderers. It was above average for that type of movie, and opened to good reviews from critics and good financial returns at the box office besides.

John also appeared in several television series including "Emergency," "Owen Marshall" and "Medical

Center." He also made lots more commercials. By the time John audition for "Kotter," he had built up a lot of acting credits on both coasts.

As John once told an interviewer, his show business career wasn't always smooth sailing. "Frankly, the only disappointment I've had out here was a couple of years back. I was up for the part of the young sailor on his way to prison in *The Last Detail*. Also auditioning was Randy Quaid, who ultimately got the part. Although it was a great role and I wanted it very much, Quaid physically looked the part. He *was* that guy. I would have had to act out the role, but I'm sure I could have done just as well."

Not getting that role in *The Last Detail* was a disappointment to John, but he's well aware of how lucky he has been to have had only one disappointment in his career. For the most part, John's rise to the top has gone extremely well. He couldn't, and doesn't, complain!

Everyone in America was talking about Vinnie Barbarino and the "sweathogs" when John made his second horror movie *Carrie*, directed by Brian de Palma. In this film he co-starred with Sissy Spacek and Nancy Allen.

In *Carrie*, John plays a real heavy named Billy Nolan who pulls a lot of dirty tricks with his girlfriend (played by Nancy) on a strange girl with mysterious powers (played by Sissy). But bad-guy Nolan gets his during the final minutes of the film. Even though he played a bad guy, John says he found the work even more exciting than the role he played in *The Devil's Rain*.

Tony Manero (John Travolta) strikes out at his parents' constant harassment in this emotional scene from *Saturday Night Fever*.
Photo Trends

Of course, he had a much larger role in *Carrie*.

But the film that skyrocketed John Travolta to stardom was *Saturday Night Fever*. He literally danced his way to the stars, with his lovely leading lady Karen Gorney.

John Travolta and Karen Gorney practicing a dance step in *Saturday Night Fever*. Wide World Photos

John no longer doubts whether audiences are responding to him or the character he's portraying. He has described Tony Manero, the part he plays in *Saturday Night Fever* as someone who "wants something more out of life than his surroundings offer him. He knows he has the potential to go ahead, but he doesn't know how. He has a fear that his life is crumbling." Needless to say, these aren't problems John is experiencing himself.

The only problems John had with filming *Saturday Night Fever* were losing 25 pounds and learning to smoke, something he has always avoided. ("I haven't any vices at all," he explains.)

In April 1978, *Time* magazine featured John as its cover story. While admitting "no one can fully define star quality," the article said John "has the moves, the presence, the princely mystique." *Time* also said *Saturday Night Fever* has started Travolta along a yellow-brick show-biz road that

Finally, the moment they had been waiting for — the Disco championship in *Saturday Night Fever*. Photo Trends

reaches out of sight. . . ." John's fans know that he really started along that "show-biz road" when he was only 12, but no one knows how far it will reach!

His fans are again enjoying John's "princely mystique," in the $6 million film version of *Grease*, which was released this summer. John doesn't

After a night of soul searching, Tony Manero (John Travolta) returns to Stephanie's (Karen Gorney) Manhattan apartment. Photo Trends

play the supporting role of "Doodie," however, but sings and dances the lead role of "Danny Zuko," with fabulous Olivia Newton-John as his leading lady.

Like Vinnie Barbarino and Tony

Manero, Danny Zuko is the leader of the pack. He's hip and handsome and goes with the prettiest girl in school. He's the one all the other gang members look up to, the one who calls the shots. In many ways *Grease* has been a lucky show for John, and the film version is bringing even more fans to the box offices than *Saturday Night Fever*!

Grease and *Saturday Night Fever* are part of a three-picture deal between John and the Robert Stigwood organization. A package that promises John more than $1 million and a percentage of the profits.

John says it's not true that he's already a millionaire, but that he ". . .could be a millionaire within the next couple of years. In the meantime," he adds happily, "I love the publicity that makes me out to be one, *now*. It's

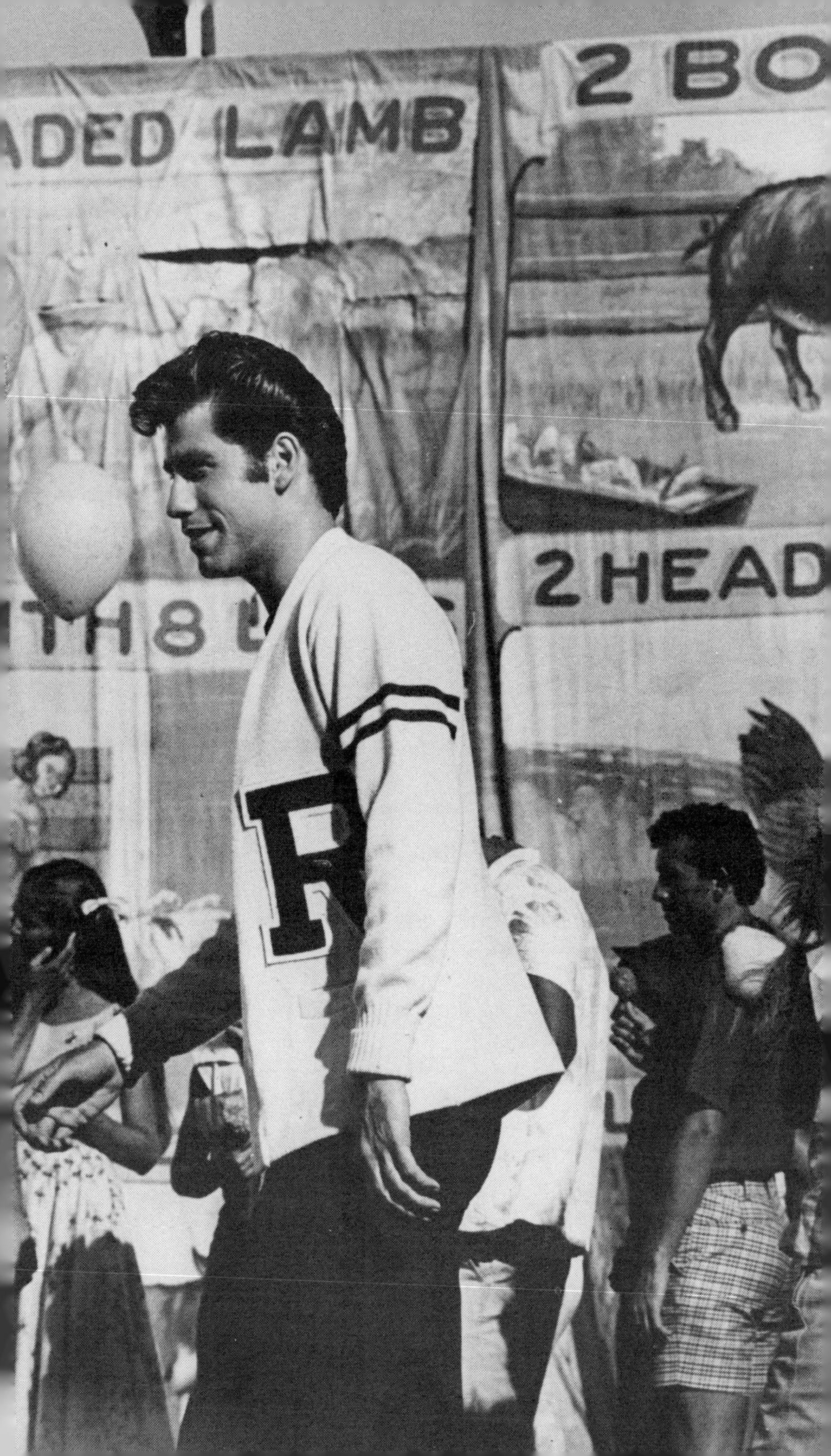

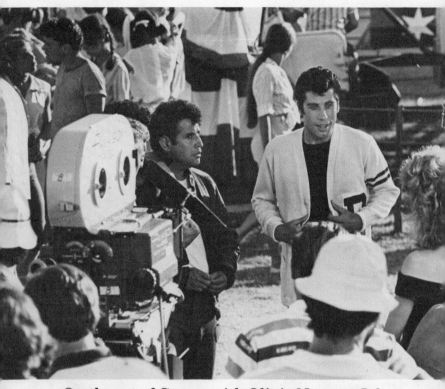

On the set of *Grease* with Olivia Newton-John and crew and cast members. Steve Schatzberg - Globe Photos

fun to see your future spread out in front of you."

In eight years, John Travolta has managed to perform in every phase of show business: He's appeared off Broadway, on Broadway, and in summer stock. In TV he's done guest roles, variety shows, more than 40 commercials, and a highly-successful weekly series. He's made some great motion pictures, as well as the made-for-television movie *The Boy In The Plastic Bubble*, which was the first major test of his dramatic talent.

John Travolta also has a personal life that he keeps very separate from his public life. The relationship which grew during the filming of *The Boy In The Plastic Bubble* and ended so tragically while John was filming *Saturday Night Fever* was to be the first major test of John Travolta, the man.

CHAPTER
6
On The Personal Side

W omen are one of John's favorite subjects. He talks a lot about romance and how he feels about dating and marriage. He says although he considers himself normally aggressive, he isn't as self-confident as he might seem, at least not where women are concerned. "I have confidence in the proper areas of my life," he says, "in my work, for example. But it doesn't slip over into my personal life."

"I've only had romances with three girls so far in my life," he recalls. "But don't forget the first time I fell for a girl, I was only 15. I started young, but my progress has been slow!"

"I met the first girl in the New Jersey high school where we both went," John says. "For five years I was with her, never going out with another girl. That's pretty hard to do when you're a teenager and want to see what's around, but I thought ours was a life-time thing."

Even after John left school the two were together most of the time. "However," John remembers, "things changed when I got into the road company of the musical *Grease*. Our relationship couldn't take the separation."

Soon after his first romance broke up, John got involved with Marilu

Marilu Henner and John Travolta practice a dance step. Nate Cutler - Globe Photos

Henner, a dancer in *Grease*. John saw her every day, and before long, the two were a very together team. "We went steady for a while and I thought I was crazy about her," but it never reached the serious stage. "We went together during the run of the play, but when the play was over, so was our relationship." However, they still remain good friends.

During the filming of *The Boy In The Plastic Bubble*, John fell in love with his co-star Diana Hyland. When she died in his arms of cancer at the age of 41, John felt as though his own life had ended. "I have never been more in love with anyone in my life," he admits unhesitatingly. "I thought I was in love before, but I wasn't."

Though John knew the exquisite actress he loved was a cancer victim, neither knew she was going to die until a few weeks before it happened. "I had more fun with Diana than I ever had in my life," John says. "And the odd thing is just before we met, I thought I would never have a successful relationship. She told me that she, too, had thought the same thing. Then, bam!"

This tragedy occurred while John was filming *Saturday Night Fever*. Its director, John Badham, told *Time* magazine that, "He put his attention to the work and overcame his emotional feelings. Some of the best scenes in the movie were done during that period." John credits Scientology with helping him cope with this personal tragedy.

John has recently said "I still want

John was very much in love with actress Diana Hyland. Her unexpected death devastated him. Here they are pictured with Diana's son. Photo by Julian Wasser

to get married, as soon as I find the right person. And I want kids, lots of them. I love them."

However, this is the same John Travolta who says, "You see, I'm only in love with my career at the moment. I'd like to marry someday, but now is not the time. I'm married strictly to my career." He wants what he wants, but only when he wants it. Still, there's no question John isn't looking as hard as he once was. Some friends say this is because of the sad way his romance with Diana Hyland ended. Nowadays he's been playing the field, cooling it, before settling into a more permanent relationship.

John's ideal woman would have to like the casual, relaxed life-style he's so crazy about. No matter what, it's a rare sight to see him wearing an outfit that doesn't include blue jeans. He's a very relaxed, California-style guy, and dressing up isn't one of his ideas of a good time.

Jeans are the perfect outfit for John since he likes to spend so much time doing things that could get his clothes dirty, like tinkering around with his motorcycle. He's definitely the wash-and-wear type.

As a result of his popularity in *Saturday Night Fever*, John has become a fashion trend-setter. The three-piece suits he danced in during that movie are now seen in and out of disco houses across the country. The tight-fitting trousers and open-necked shirts certainly show off John's terrific physique to a great advantage. And his fans want to look as good as he does!

So John may be wash-and-wear at

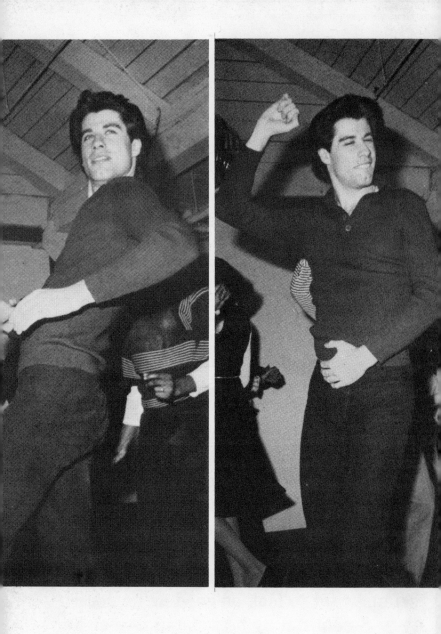

John getting into a disco mood in his own inimitable way! Photos by Bob Deutsch

home, in worn jeans and tee-shirts, but his public image is that of a snappy dresser—a real cool dude.

John lives in the Los Angeles suburb of West Hollywood, right on the fringe of Beverly Hills. He has a splendid one-bedroom apartment in a high-rise building with a perfect view of the city and the craggy hills of the San Fernando Mountains. The apartment is filled with John's collections, accumulated over the years. Many are antiques. Most are related to his interest in aviation.

It's impossible not to notice his love of airplanes immediately upon entering his home. There are models all over the place! Some hang from the ceiling; others stand propped on shelves. Where there aren't airplanes, there are books; volume after volume on every facet of aviation. He reads and rereads them.

John began taking flying lessons at

16. He now has his private pilot's license, which insurance companies won't let him use since he's a "million-dollar property." His first plane was an Aircoupe, a single-engine, two-seater. Now John's got a DC-3 which is big enough for his family and the families of all the other "sweathogs," too.

John was always sports-minded in school, and today his interest in athletics remains. His six-foot, 170-pound body is in great shape. He's kept it that way in part through his love of tennis. Tennis is *the* sport in southern California. It seems as if practically everyone plays or is learning to play. Even people who have never handled a tennis racquet before soon become devotees of the game after settling in the Los Angeles area.

Not only does John look good wearing tennis whites, he also has just the right kind of lean, long-legged body to be an excellent player. And, as all tennis buffs know, this is the kind of game that gives every muscle in the body a complete workout.

When he's not returning volleys on the tennis court, John can be found on another kind of court. He's a big basketball fan. John played basketball in high school, and he loves to play whenever he has some spare time. It's not at all unusual to find him shooting a few baskets.

John also uses his athletic ability to lend a hand at charity basketball games. There are quite a few of these in Hollywood every year. Celebrities like Elliott Gould, James Caan, Henry Winkler, Desi Arnaz, Jr., Dino Martin, Michael Landon, Gabriel Kaplan, and John Travolta get together to play non-celebrity teams, usually made up of professional basketball players or other athletic groups, such as the Beverly Hills Police Department. Everyone has a good time and all proceeds from the ticket sales go to charity.

John loves food almost as much as he loves sports and usually works off all those extra calories. He likes all kinds of food, but is especially fond of Chinese dishes.

John's also into cars and bikes. He's got a motorcycle and can often be seen zooming through the Hollywood canyons. The car John usually drives isn't exactly new, but it's mighty special. It's a classic 1955 Thunderbird that he keeps in top shape. It's a beauty and he's crazy about it.

When he just wants to relax at home, John likes nothing better than sitting around playing guitar, often singing along with his music. Everyone

Enjoying an evening out with Lily Tomlin.
Photo by Bob Deutsch

who's heard John's singing in the hit *Grease* knows what a good voice he has.

What else is John into? He's a big fan of James Cagney, Marlon Brando, Paul Newman, Robert DeNiro, Cloris Leachman and Ellen Burstyn.

John's favorite pop singer is Barbra Streisand. Musically, he prefers the classics. "I don't like contemporary music that well," he says. "Some country and western is interesting. My taste is not a set thing — whatever appeals to me at the time."

What appeals to John at this time is working with Lily Tomlin on *Moment To Moment*, the third film of his current movie contact. As far as his future with the "sweathogs," John says, "I'll play 'Kotter' as long as they need and want me. But someday we're all going to outgrow our parts. How long can you play a 16-year-old?" But John also refers to "Kotter" as his "first and last TV series," and he'd welcome the chance to get out of his contract. "Still," he insists, "I never knock Vinnie. He broke me through the sound barrier."

Only in his mid-twenties, John Travolta looks back on his career and says, "It couldn't have happened more naturally for me." He's totally pleased with where he's at and what he's doing. At the same time, he doesn't feel all that awed or overwhelmed by his super-stardom.

"My big break was bound to happen," John explains. "I spent years planning for it. But if success had come earlier, I doubt if I would have been able to handle it. Scientology has helped me cope with the pressure and responsibility I now find in my life. I don't have a swelled head, either, and I suppose a man in my position could easily become egotistical."

In general, John's attitude about life these days is relaxed and easygoing. He doesn't even mind the high pressure that is involved in being someone constantly in the public eye. He admits he doesn't have time for a lot of his hobbies lately, but adds, "That's okay. I've got plenty of time for that."

John couldn't be more pleased with his popularity. "I'm just excited. I'm getting a lot of respect as an actor from it. You know, not just as a teen idol, which is fun, but I'm getting respect as an actor. And that's nice.

"I'm enjoying my success," he says, "and for the first time in my life, nothing seems out of reach. It's a strange, but good feeling to be able to have anything I want—to be able to reach out and take what I desire."

Yet for all his success, for all the praise, John remains the same person he was before. He hasn't let go of his head. He hasn't let it make him hard to deal with.

More than half of John Travolta is unspoiled, and well-meaning. John is the kind of young man every girl's parents would be happy to see their daughter going off on a date with.

And the women John dates always speak highly of him. He is a real old-fashioned gentleman, they'll tell you. He respects women yet never treats them as if they were helpless and frail. He has a real understanding of women and appreciates their feelings. No one can remember him exhibiting any chauvinistic attitudes—and for good reason: the many women in his immediate family taught him early in life that women are every bit as bright, interesting and capable of achievement as men.

John has summed up his own

wishes for the future by stating, "Personally, I'd like to get married and have a family someday. Professionally, I only wish for myself to be able to do all three—Broadway, movies and television—and to really make a go of it. So far it's really been so perfect, being able to do all three, that it's very exciting. I think that's the way a career should go."

John is a great-looking guy who likes his parents, frowns on drugs, takes his profession seriously, likes to have a good time, enjoys the company of the opposite sex, and has his own goals and values. He's a man with few surprises up his sleeve. When it comes to success stories, John's is one of the most gratifying.

John is enjoying the freedom success is bringing to him. He's had heartache in his personal life, but his professional life has no limits. He can now do what he wants, when he wants to do it. And who wouldn't like that?

Yes, John has his own future pretty well figured out. He says he wouldn't care if his stardom ended. "It's nice having people know who I am," he admits. "I would like to have the recognition continue forever, but if anything happens and it doesn't last, it won't tear me apart. I'm enjoying the glow, but I know it could end anytime."

John has many important things planned for his future, and he'll do them all, each and every one of them, when he feels the time is right. This very talented actor will be around for a long, long time.